Spotlig... *Poets*

The Gift of Perception

  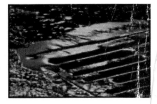

Edited by Sarah Marshall

Spotlight Poets

First published in Great Britain in 2004 by
SPOTLIGHT POETS
Remus House
Coltsfoot Drive
Peterborough
PE2 9JX
Telephone: 01733 898102
Fax: 01733 313524
Website: www.forwardpress.co.uk

SB ISBN 1 84077 110 0

Foreword

As a nation of poetry writers and lovers, many of us are still surprisingly reluctant to go out and actually buy the books we cherish so much. Often when searching out the work of newer and less known authors it becomes a near impossible mission to track down the sort of books you require. In an effort to break away from the endless clutter of seemingly unrelated poems from authors we know nothing or little about; Spotlight Poets has opened up a doorway to something quite special.

The Gift of Perception is a collection of poems to be cherished forever; featuring the work of twelve captivating poets each with a selection of their very best work. Placing that alongside their own personal profile gives a complete feel for the way each author works, allowing for a clearer idea of the true feelings and reasoning behind the poems.

The poems and poets have been chosen and presented in a complementary anthology that offers a variety of ideals and ideas, capable of moving the heart, mind and soul of the reader.

Sarah Marshall

Contents

Auntie Glen. (Sennybridge)

Ron Bissett

David Russell

The Authors
& Poems

Antony John Boughton

Hi. Let me introduce myself. My name is Antony John Boughton, but prefer to be known as Tony. I am 35 years of age, recently married to Mandy, with three children of my own and three further step-children. I live in the village of Bradwell, near Great Yarmouth in Norfolk.

I was born in Dunstable, Bedfordshire, and moved to East Anglia at the age of fourteen. Throughout my childhood my only ambition was to be a professional footballer (well, tell me a young lad that doesn't!). I made it as far as having trials with Luton Town but the dream ended there. Football, and especially Luton Town, remain my passion as well as my dog, 'Umbro', and listening to rock music, namely 'Queen', 'Def Leppard' and more recently, 'The Darkness'.

You can imagine my surprise, and that of everybody else, when I finally ended up in medicine, and qualified as a Registered General Nurse in 1992. From there I joined the Royal Navy in April of that year and served four years at Royal Naval Hospital, Haslar, in Gosport, Hants.

I have been writing poetry for as long as I can remember but only recently had the nerve to send my work to Forward Press in the hope it would get recognition, and up to now I have had four poems published. I tend to write about life, love, and generally things that have happened to myself and nearest and dearest. I continue to write mainly for pleasure, but in the future hope for further recognition.

Thank you for your interest and reading the above.

Alcohol

I get into your veins
I'm always by your side
I'm there when you sleep
When your eyes open wide

Do I really help you?
Am I friend or foe?
Do you really care?
Do you really know?

Am I a poison
Or am I sweet?
Are the expectations
The ones I meet?

If you just let me
I'll get under your skin
Then just think
The state you'll be in!

Don't Give Up

Although life's been a struggle
And we've dealt with so much
We're meant to be together
To cuddle, hug and touch

If our love isn't worth fighting for
And it seems too much to try
Will we both feel any better
When the tears have all dried?

When our time is finally up
And when we come to call
Could you always sleep at night
Knowing you gave your all?

So when you feel despondent
And feel you're wasting time
Just hang in there together
And we will be just fine.

Father's Day

A day to celebrate being a dad
Even if your kids are away
A day to be happy instead of sad
And keep the tears at bay

It's hoping the letterbox goes
And a card falls on the floor
But reality says it just won't happen
You've been here too often before

It's the day you realise the mistakes you've made
Have robbed you of this day
Instead of waking with your kids
Your thoughts are far away

You envy the dads who have their breakfast
Brought to them in bed
You dream of what it must be like
But it's easier to dismiss it instead

So put on a smile and try to enjoy
What the day is for
It's only twenty-four hours out of the year
And there will be many more

So instead of feeling envy
Of luckier dads than I
I'll pretend it doesn't matter
And silent tears I'll cry.

Heroes

*(Dedicated to the sailors, airmen and troops
who will never return home)*

You left these British shores
To fight in a foreign land
Now you're not coming home
Your blood is on ﹍   ﹍

But tonight there will be tea﹍ ﹍
From your children and wives
You believed in the cause
And for that gave your lives

The Iraqis will have freedom
The regime blown apart
The pride of your loved ones
Will always fill their hearts

You fought with guile and strength
No weakness did you show
Your country very proud of you
That you ought to know

For each one of you not coming home
Thousands you have saved
Thank you for being British
Thank you for being brave.

Isolation

I feel so isolated
So very alone
No one to talk to
At the end of a phone

It's all in my control
All a state of mind
But why is happiness
So very hard to find?

Always there for everyone else
But where are they for me?
My so-called good friends
Are just another fantasy

Who needs them anyway?
I'll sort it on my own
Anyway, I'm kind of getting used
To being all alone.

Life

What is the point of life
And why are we really here?
Is it something to cherish
Or something to be feared?

Do we make our own luck
Or fate throw its own hand?
Are we really in control
Do we really understand?

Should we live day to day
Or can the future be planned?
Can we look beyond tomorrow
Is it out of our own hands?

Do we rejoice at each new day
Or fear what it might hold?
Should we believe our own eyes
Or swallow what we're told?

Who controls our lives anyway?
Who makes all the rules?
Is it Big Brother and the banks?
Are we really the puppet fools?

My Children

They are my morning chorus, setting sun
The apples of my eye
The stars in the black expanse
The tears when I cry

The reasons that I wake
Give me strength throughout the day
And when I lose the path ahead
The lights that show the way

My lighthouse on a treacherous sea
In a storm, my safe port
Forever in my heart
And forever in my thoughts

They make me laugh when I'm down
Make me happy instead of sad
And I only hope they know
I'm so proud to be their dad

November 5th

Reflection on their faces
As the bonfire comes alive
Full of anticipation
As they look towards the skies

Colours dancing everywhere
The looks of disbelief
A rainbow in the Heavens
A falling autumnal leaf

Aroma of the chestnuts
As they roast upon the fire
The merriment of adults
As the kids begin to tire

The token barbecue
Everyone's had their fill
The children wanting their warm beds
Dad is feeling ill

The evening is drawing to a close
People drift off home
The solitary Catherine wheel that wouldn't light

Sits there all alone

One Year On

(Dedicated to the best ever stepdad)

How time flies
And life just goes on
Look over my shoulder
And twelve months have gone

Not a day goes by
Without a thought of you
But now more happy thoughts
And the tears becoming few

I remember your love
Your kindness and support
I remember our secrets
And never getting caught

If I could be just half the man
And be loved as much too
Then my kids would be so proud of me
As I was knowing you

So, wherever you are
And whatever you do
Thanks for always being there
Thanks for being you

Serenity

Where the sky meets the sea
And the gulls dare to fly
The dawning of a new day
As the sun climbs in the sky

When the waves are crashing round
Like surround sound that's turned on
Close your eyes for a second
And all your troubles are gone

As the wind starts with baited breath
The swirling of the sands
At that precious moment
The world is in your hands

As the wind and waves meet
The crescendo of the sound
Just for that fleeting time
Serenity you've found

The Constant

It's always there
Doesn't go away
The constant pain
You feel each day

It may be physical
Or mental too
All you know
Is it won't leave you

The constant aching
Why is it there?
I don't want it
It's just not fair

Is there a reason?
What have I done?
I pray to God
It will soon be gone

Turn To You

(For Mandy)

When my heart is bleeding
With the troubles in my life
I turn to you for guidance
My darling, loving wife

If it's falling apart
And there's nothing I can do
When I lack the strength
That's when I turn to you

If there is an answer
But I don't know how or where
If I can't find it by myself
I know that you are there

Unknown Heroes

It's not only Superheroes
That wear capes and suits
Don't have to move mountains
Or wear red boots

They don't need the strength
Of a steaming train
Or a fist the size
Of an elephant's brain

A hero is someone
Who's touched you inside
But you should have told them
Before they died

You were my heroes
Will always be
And though you're not here
I know you're there for me

When

When will you believe
You are not second-best?
You're one in a million
Better than all the rest

When will you believe
You are truly loved?
Since I've met you
I thank the Heavens above

When will you believe
I fancy you daft?
The way that you move
The way you make me laugh

When will you believe
You're the one for me?
Let the future unfold
What will be will be

When will you believe?
Together forever
Nothing else matters
Lose you never

You

My friend, my lover
My reason to live
My joy, my laughter
My love I give

My shoulder to cry on
When things look bleak
No need to pretend
With you I can be weak

You hold the keys
To all my dreams
The future so bright
Or so it seems

When we're apart
You are on my mind
The strength within
You allow me to find

I'll never let you
Walk away
It's in the stars
With me, you'll stay

Jackie Jones-Cahill

My name is Jackie Jones-Cahill and London is my home, although there is Irish blood from my sweet mother's side of the family. I am forty-four years old. I am a mother and a grandmother.

I started writing after the loss of my mum in 2001 and my father seven months later in 2002. My mum died of lung cancer and my father also died of cancer. I, too, had cancer but it was caught in time. I have suffered miscarriages and I went through a dreadful form of bullying when I was younger. These tragedies brought out all my feelings in my writing. My poetry is helping me to cope a little better and if I can help another to cope by my poetry that will make me a very happy person . . .

My cousin, Maria Ann Cahill, has been a great support to me, encouraging me to write, and offering advice after our many long talks. She tells me to keep going even when it's hard. She was the person who first introduced me to the poetry field.

Since then I have written so many poems straight from the heart and I can tell you that this does help me cope and it is wonderful to share my writing with others. I had never written before.

I have some work being published on the 31st March by Anchor Books. This is a wonderfully exciting time for me as I embark upon the poetry of my heart.

Soshh!

My mother says, 'Soshh!
Don't cry, dry your eyes,
I'm only up in the sky,
I'm sorry I had to die,
I had cancer, that's why,
But I'll always love you,
I'll watch over you,
I'm sorry I died.'

Losing

The pain of losing babies,
Is more than I can stand,
I didn't see his face,
Or get to hold his hand,
I can't get this thought out of my head,
How can my tiny baby be dead?

Terminator

Our cat has started to wee inside,
Is it too cold to go outside?
I've put him out, he cried,
'Please let me come back inside,
It's because I'm old and cold,
Please don't scold!'

Terminator's Second Story

He looks at me with big green eyes,
I know he's saying he's tired,
But my house now smells,

What about my pride?
Will they think it's me?
I want to run and hide,
Come on Termie, please try!
Do not wee inside.

Tick-Tock

I love grandfather clocks,
But mine doesn't go tick-tock,
The clock is electric,
It has three shelves.

A secret compartment,
Which holds all my heartfelt
Letters and poems for my parents,
When my heart broke.

Falling Into Bits

It only takes a few minutes,
To save you falling into bits,
Having a smear isn't much fun,
But sometimes you have to think of number one,
You got the 'all clear',
Now it is all done!

An Angel

My mother is an angel,
Sometimes I feel her watching me,
Does she get lonely,
Not being able to talk to me?
I'm just thankful,
That she is watching over me.

Clever

Bullies think they are so clever,
Picking on people no matter the weather,
We should stand together,
Sticking up for ourselves is hard to do,
But a little love will get us through,
So go away bullies we won't cry, 'Boo-hoo!'

Is It Hereditary?

I went for a smear,
It wasn't necessary,
But I was glad,
For I had got to stage three,

It was cancer, you see,
All in twelve weeks,
It came to be,

Now they tell me it's hereditary,
Do you know your medical history,
Or will you end up like me?

Little White Stick

I watched my mum die in agony,
Then to be told it was a cigarette, you see,
How has that little white stick affected me?
Having no mum has broken me!

Horse And Cart

My mum had a beautiful horse and cart,
That's how her funeral had to start

I gave her a kiss, I placed a letter,
No pain, no tablets, no cancer

But leaving us all behind did matter

But I couldn't watch her get any sadder
So rest in peace and climb that ladder

To get into Heaven where life will be better
And when it's our time we will all be together.

Nuns

My mum was brought up by nuns,
Sometimes she got bored and wanted to run,
She went there when she was young,
With her sister, Phill,
As their mother was very ill,
Unfortunately their mother died,
So Phill and my mum stayed together,
Always by each other's side,
Now even in Heaven,
As they have both died.

David William Hill

Born 19th March 1932, son of a coalminer, in Neath, Glamorgan, South Wales. We had a poor but loving home. My father and mother were strong Baptists and I attended a Sunday school of 200 girls and boys.

I attended Gnoll Infants school then passed my 11 + for the Neath Intermediate School (now Grammar), fee-paying £3 6s 8d per term!

1944 - free education and Health Service thanks to Rab Butler and Aneurin Bevan and of course the Second World War.

On leaving school in 1948 I worked as an office boy in The Briton Ferry Steel Company, when my father was forced to retire with pneumoconiosis (20% coal dust in his lungs). I had achieved 2 credits in Maths and physics and passes in English language and literature, Welsh, economics and history. It was called The School Certificate of the Central Welsh Board.

I was then conscripted into the Royal Army Pay Corps for two years, volunteering for overseas service. 13 months were spent in Command Pay Office, Kure, Japan, having sailed on the Empire Medway, calling at Port Said (Suez), Aden, Colombo, Singapore, Hong Kong and finally Kure (about six weeks in all) Saw Tokyo, Osaka, Yokohama, but worst of all Hiroshima, six years after the first atomic bomb. The utter devastation, the shadows on the walls where people had been sitting and the dust we breathed had its effect on me, having to spend a month in hospital, which I do not remember. This was the start, I think, of mental illness which has dogged me throughout my life.

Back to Blighty, my old job gone, I worked as a pay clerk for The Slag Reduction Company, Briton Ferry, whose rugby team I played for. In 1953 I entered St Luke's College, Exeter, University of the South West. Achieved diploma in Physical Education - Health Ed. Anatomy and Physiology, swimming, life-saving etc. English Language and literature, Divinity, maths and played rugby for the College.

I got married in Exeter in 1955 and we had four children by 1963.

In 1959 received Commission in Royal Navy as an Instructor Officer for six years and spent six weeks on HMS Vigo on a goodwill visit to Cuxhaven and Iceland.

My second wife lost her only baby when a few weeks old and adopted a ten-month old boy, Stephen. He was 15 when I became his step father. He had been the man of the house so there was obvious friction. Enough said!

Is Now And Ever Shall Be

I've never lived this moment before.
This moment has never lived before.
It's new, it's here, it's gone!
There's another to replace,
This state of being, this moment of grace,
This entity of time and space.
There is air, water, earth and heat.
How can we change this eternal seat?
Two hundred years from now, we'll all be dead!
So why hasten that state by planning ahead?
The use of wasteful weaponry,
The goal of pointless bloodshed?
Why not live in the present time and space,
For its beauty, love and grace?
The true way of life, and rationality face?
Why be in conflict with another's son,
When we have given to us the only one,
Which we are, in our essence, bound to be,
By our image, our birth, our eternity?
In this moment prepare for the moments ahead,
But not for stupid strife, foolish fear,
Or evil wars - may these remain dead!
Use your head, and think thoughts
That become actions,
For each to be fed with the true bread.
Remember, 'I am with you always,' He said.

My Secret

Enclosed within each 'I'
Is a secret *'me'*
Which is kept from every other,
Sister or brother, father and mother.
But we cannot hide anything
From the self.
Especially the *'Greater Self'*,
Creator of, in the first place, the 'I'.
His or her name is God or 'I Am'

God's Son's Earthly name is Jesus of Nazareth,
Who said, 'I am the Way, the Truth and the Life.'
That is, your life and mine!
For His gifts to us are divine.
There is no doubt that
Jesus became 'The Christ'
And in all humility,
His strong advice
To *all* is to ascend, not descend
Or *fall*.
So we must realise and recognise,
And reconcile
Our lives to Him, who gives us our *all*.

    Addendum: Christ has died
                    Christ is risen
                    He *has come again*
                    To a chosen few (eg the Apostles, St Paul)
                    And *will* come to *all* who believe in Him.

The Life Of Death

What is the purpose of death?
He said, 'Unless a seed falls to the ground
It cannot grow and bear fruit.'
We delight in death, and in killing abound.
What blossoms forth to suit
The killer or his Maker?
Good or infertile ground?
Blessed tree or bomb crater?
The certainty of life
Is that it ends in death,
But only of the body.
Though even that transforms to new life.
The life of the soul and spirit
Goes on to inherit
The reward of torment
Resulting from Earth's loss
Or beneficial bent.
We can prepare for death
As we can prepare for the rest of our life
Doing good and 'saving' in the belief
That abundance is for all,
Not struggle and strife!
Giving to and forgiving our fellows,
It follows, we shall bear fruit richly,
And gathering rosebuds while we may,
We will promulgate peace
And progress indefinitely.

Mine Or Yours (Landmines Or Flowers)

Could terrorists exist
Without arms?
Could gunmen persist
Without guns?
Demolition of all weaponry
Destruction of all armoury
Would halt the terrorist cause
At source.
No bombs or missiles
To wreak plunder,
No 'force' to part asunder.
We could start to enjoy
The world's wonder.
Let us beat guns
Into ploughshares,
Turn tanks into tractors,
Resolve argument with peace affairs
Evolve our amicable factors.
Let us not say,
'This planet is ours,
To possess, to have'
But 'The Earth, with its growth
Or removal, is the Lord's,
And the fullness thereof.'

Worship

How can we follow a Cross?
It is made of wood from a tree.
We must follow Him
Who hung on the Cross,
For you and for me!
He was made of flesh and blood,
And bones spaced severally.
To follow the Cross
Means worshipping a symbol,
A wood or golden idol.
To worship our Lord,
Means loving 'man', God's minstrel.
The lack of love in our world
Is due to worshipping the cudgel,
The flail, the whip, the weapon.
We must worship the Son,
The real being, God,
Not any man-made icon.
We are to seek and find,
To ask and receive,
To knock, the door to unchain,
And with open and pure mind
To not ourselves deceive
But, Hope, Faith and Love attain.

Life

'Christ is the Way,
The Truth and the Life',
Whose life?
All life, yours and mine,
Ultimately divine.
We are in Him,
He is in us.
Life is the kingdom within,
At one with God,
The Creator of life,
Who is where all lives end and begin.
Christ made life to be
Or not to be,
As you like it,
Measure for measure,
In Tempest or Caesar
Enacted for the pleasure
Of Himself and all.
It is now and forever.
Feel alive, bravely strive,
For all life is 'one'
And ends never.

Existence

To exist,
A thing must have been.
We persist,
Nothing comes from nothing.
All life is preceded by life.
How can anything
Be a 'something'
Without previous cause?
The 'effect' is the result,
The form shaped from its source
So the beginning is the 'cause'.
But also the 'effect' of a former state.
Like the amoeba
It develops out of itself,
But there must be a cause
For the amoeba's initial being.
To learn about 'cause' and 'effect',
We can study history,
But the origin of 'time'
And the infinity of 'space'
Remain a mystery,
Hidden, thank Heaven,
In deepest secrecy.

Creation

The Sun gave birth
To the Earth
Out of the Moon.
As soon as Earth was born
The Sun made dawn,
And the Moon made eventide,
Nightfall follows
Day and all life wallows
Static and moving
In a cosmology
Of light and learning.
The Earth bears her progeny -
Man and a miscellany,
But all is kept striving
By the Sun and Moon giving
Life and sustenance
To the growing and achieving
Mineral, plant, animal
And human kingdom.
When we learn to receive
And acknowledge and realise
The nature of being,
We will become ultimately wise,
And from ignorance arise
To measure and treasure
And take great pleasure
In that partly veiled prize.

A Child's Enquiry

'Where do I come from, Uncle Jack?
Has there always, always been *me*?
Am I a candle blown, or an empty gown,
Or a cut-off, chopped-down tree?
I want to know, for I care, Uncle Jack,
For those who will follow me.
Are they now dead, waiting to be born,
Those of the future world?
Or do they exist in a spirit form,
In a vast womb, cocooned and curled?'
'Yes, you come from a sphere, my dear,
A state of 'becoming to be'.
You're not a candle blown, or an empty gown,
Or a cut-off chopped-down tree.
Some day you'll know, as you are known.
Some day, you'll see!'

1984

Big Brother is watching you.
He's also watching over you.
He's not a tyrant,
But a servant.
Not a disaster,
But a master.
Not a compeller,
But a persuader,
A guide, a helper, a source.
Where does He dwell?
In every cell,
In every heart and soul.
He's our life force.
Acknowledge Him or not,
He's all we've got!

The Present Moment

This time, now,
Is the after-life
Of all time past.
This time, now,
Is the pre-existence
Of all time to be.
So past, present and future
Resolve and unify
In this moment, now.
What we do now
Is determined by the past.
What we do now
Determines the future.
How long will life last?
Forever and ever -
As it was, so it is,
And ever shall be,
World without end
Or beginning,
Full of true and
Real meaning.
Look to what is now.
Do what is to be done.
Nothing is new,
Yet all is striving
To become as and at one,
Under the radiant,
Life-giving, all-feeding Sun.
The Light of the world, the Sun,
And the Light of the world, the Son
Are inseparably and initially 'One',
As when all begun.

Esther Annette Davies

I am a sixty-two year old Welsh lady who is very proud of her heritage.

My husband and I have been married for forty-three years and have a lovely daughter and son-in-law and two wonderful grandchildren.

I have been very unfortunate, health-wise, with too many complaints to bore you with but I will say, after experiencing several strokes some years ago and undergoing a life-threatening vascular surgery operation, I turned to poetry and family history as a means of therapy, and also to overcome the stress and depression brought on by the after-effects of the operation.

Prior to this unfortunate period in my life, I never had the inclination or, as wrongly thought, the ability to put pen to paper in this way.

In retrospect, I must admit writing poetry has not only been therapeutic but has given me many hours of pleasure. The acclaim I have received from friends and family has certainly made it all worthwhile.

I like to write on topical subjects and things about which I feel deeply.

Sister Bernadine

I saw a vision kneeling there,
     her head was bowed in silent prayer.
Silver hair and an enchanting smile,
     to visit the sick walking many a mile.

She left her homeland to serve the Lord,
     helping the less fortunate is her reward.
If there be saints, let her be one,
     in appreciation of the work she's done.

Sweet Mary and your Saviour Son,
     look down with love on this precious nun.
Please ease her work and make her rest,
     we love her dearly, she's one of the best!

Our Dear Friend Richard

Our dear friend Richard,
loves travel I've heard.
But I know in his heart,
he is quite a home bird.

He knows that it's travel,
that broadens the mind.
But his longing for Wales,
makes it one of a kind.

The wondrous mountains,
with snow on their peaks.
And the rain in our shoes,
that makes funny squeaks.

The song of old miners,
with melodious sound.
Some gave up their lives,
to dig coal underground.

We all love the valleys,
with their myths and old tales.
So remember the saying,
'There's no place like Wales'.

This rhyme is for Richard,
who is one of the best.
He's always been special,
above all the rest.

Remember Your Roots

Do you ever feel threatened,
by toffs and upstarts?
Well, don't be, they're bullies,
all talk and no hearts.

Give me a person,
who is true to their roots.
Not a pebble-mouthed speaker,
with airs and posh boots.

I never feel awkward,
or try to act grand.
I am proud of my accent,
background and land.

My parents worked hard,
their values were high.
We were taught to be proud,
and never to lie.

Life can be cruel,
don't think you're too grand.
To help the less fortunate,
just hold out a hand.

Your reward will be heartfelt,
a smile in sad eyes.
Helping those who have nothing,
all riches denied.

Playing At Twickers

We're all off to Twickers,
To cheer on our lads.
You must beat the English,
And make our hearts glad.

We have a new coach,
Let's give him your best.
Score plenty of tries,
Let Jones' boot do the rest.

Don't take us for granted,
Rugby's in all our blood.
It's part of our heritage,
We thrive in the mud.

We have talent in abundance,
In each valley or town.
Once the right team is bonded,
They will bring back the crown.

The English are playing,
With style and panache.
Get out there and prove,
The Welsh still have class.

So remember you Welsh men,
Show the world we have flare.
Take the smile off their faces,
Mock the Welsh if you dare!

Say `No` To Drugs

Say 'No!' to drugs,
They're really not cool.
They mess up your brain,
And make you a fool.

You'll lose all your dignity,
And also your looks.
Then comes the thieving,
You're now on police books.

You steal from your family,
And also your mates.
Your parents who love you,
Both know it's too late.

They'll call you a junkie,
And take a wide berth.
You're no longer a cool dude,
You're the centre of mirth.

You've now hit the bottom,
And don't want to die.
No longer a cool dude,
No time for goodbye.

Help, Not Judge

Give a thought to people,
who must leave their homes.
To live on the streets,
in gangs or alone.

Many parents reject,
their families and friends.
To buy cigs, drink and drugs,
a sure recipe to the end.

The children are sent,
to live in a home.
Where it is hoped they are cared for,
and not left alone.

They feel very rejected,
and life's not too grand.
The staff try to help,
and offer their hand.

They won't trust anybody,
just shout, rant and moan.
Wanting someone to love them,
and their very own home.

When you walk down the street,
in your lovely new gear.
Remember the young people,
who won't make it this year.

Linzy

My granddaughter Linzy,
Is special and wise.
The day she was born,
It enriched all our lives.

There's never a dull day,
When Linzy's around.
Especially when Gran,
Gives the odd fifty pounds.

But when I am low,
And I get very sad.
She puts her arms round me,
And it makes me feel glad.

But Linzy's no angel,
Her parents might think.
She won't wash the dishes,
They are still in the sink.

A normal teenager,
Like all of the rest.
Raised by two loving parents,
She'll turn out the best.

Richard

I love our Richard,
He's stolen my heart.
And I hope for a long time,
We won't have to part.

When he comes home from school,
He looks like a sweep.
If his mother could see him,
She'd just want to weep.

He says, 'Gran, stop fussing,
Can I please have my tea?
The boys will be calling,
In a minute for me.'

Now as I get older,
I sit and reflect.
I'll always love Richard,
He's one of the best.

Too Proud To Die

Please give us a change,
we all want to work.
We are proud of our foundry,
where nobody shirks.

Don't let our town die,
it's breaking our hearts,
We'll pray that Corus,
will give us a start.

We have lived with the threat,
for many a year.
I know all our wives,
will shed many a tear.

Our small town is friendly,
and parking is free.
A street market on Friday,
with bargains, you'll see.

Ebbw Vale has a history,
of great 'Labour' sons.
Like Llew, Mike and Nye Bevan,
they would fight hard, not run.

We've lost all our coal mines,
now the steelworks are doomed.
We need work in the valleys,
not a life full of gloom.

So come on Rhodri Morgan,
you must do your best.
To bring work to the valleys,
give us hope, you'll be blessed.

Help Me

As he walked the beach,
One stormy night.
He heard a voice,
And had quite a fright.

The beach was long,
Waves lashed the shore.
'Please cut me loose,
Help me go.'

He looked around,
The beach was bare.
Someone was crying,
It filled the air.

His lamp was dim,
The wind roared loud.
No moon tonight,
Just thick black cloud.

As if by magic,
He saw the net.
With a thrashing sound,
He would never forget.

His fishing knife,
Would stop those cries.
He'd cut the net,
And free its prize.

A beautiful mermaid,
With long, black hair.
Swam out to sea,
Was she really there?

Depression

I'm in a dark tunnel,
Hands pulling me down.
How long have I been here,
Far under the ground?

I hear my heart beating,
As loud as a drum.
I'm sure the end's coming,
Faint voices call, 'Come.'

Someone calls out, 'Esther,
Don't give in and die.
We'll love and protect you.'
I heave a big sigh.

'Please look up and see,
A trace of a light.
Come out of the tunnel,
Choose life, it's alright.'

I'll start at the bottom,
And turn to the light.
I've remembered the family,
'I love you, I'll fight!'

Wake Up It's Spring

Winter's cold fingers are losing their power,
The earth's started warming for spring's cheerful flowers.
Small leaves are unfolding their warm winter beds,
Flowers are peeping just showing their heads.

Spring's round the corner to comfort and cheer,
The birds are returning to sing loud and clear.
Large clumps of daffodils swaying graceful in the breeze,
Squirrels start waking in their drays in large trees.

Leave winter's depression and open your eyes,
Enjoy life's free pleasures and cloudless blue skies.
Throw off your shoes, walk barefoot in the grass,
It's a wonderful feeling, no need to have cash.

K Chesney-Woods

I am a retired professional engineer. My work experience taught me that an original design-thought resulted in extensive testing and paperwork. I began writing poetry because my object is to reduce many thoughts and descriptions into a distilled and summarised piece. This was the exact opposite to my working life and this appealed to me.

I first started writing poetry in response to an advert in the South Shields Gazette by Arrival Press of Peterborough, requesting poems in 1992. The result was that my poem 'Seagulls' about King Street seagulls was my first.

I am influenced by nature and my inspiration from detailing simple acts and scenery in the form of a poem. I have short poems which consider social conditions but keep these to myself. As the publisher knows, this year I issued a poem for my Christmas card. This was the result of a Christmas experience.

My ability was encouraged by a course on writing at night classes in Chester-le-Street. I then went on courses at Durham University. There I was successful in the following modules

The Design and Craft of Writing.

The Creative Impulse.

Contemporary Poetry and Prose.

All towards the Certificate of Continuing Education in Creative Arts.

Seagulls

South Shields King Street harsh laughing cries
Paranoiac-stirring sniggers all around you
The ultimate in sniggering seagull experience.

They are daft things wheeling and gliding above
Inspiring humans with their glamorous ways
Then all at once they down us with their fishy smell.

Shoreline mannequin parade of matching coloured bills
    and legs and feet
Fishing boat staccato surround like a stilled film frame
All rubbish by man provided inland dumps.

Delilah II

*(Or a Christmas visit to the Barbers in South Shields
the following year)*

Different barbers the following year.
These unisex ladies wore different gear.
All dressed up as Father Christmas.
Complete with shorts, thighs, what a prize!

Snip, snip, snip, snip, snip, snip.
This Christmas has
This Christmas has
Provided my own dear Stockton lass.

He Didn't Even Ask Me My Telephone Number

Would like to grace my table - empty.
With a telephone number - rare.
Would like to grace my table - rare.
With a dress more rare.

She now graces my table - always.
The use of my telephone to her - rare.
She now graces my table - always.
With a variety of dresses most rare.

Dawn

Dark red horizontalled horizon
Dark indistinct daybreak dawn
Orangeing outwards upwards
Into the still dark elevations.

Orange through the crossed myriads
Of dark trees' twigs loosely woven.
Smudgy trailing trail
Of early stoking smoke.

Vivid early spectacle
Now weakens into the general sky
The colour now diluting darkness
Spilling over in the great expanse.

Dawn; daily and seasonally
Moves its start along the skyline
Man-made movements, Dawn's an aircraft vapour trail
Earth-made movement, Dawn's the dawn.

Life's Anchor

Before the Reformation.
The 12 to 1500s

A stage is set before you.
A love story - true.
An Anker in the Anker's house.

Chester-le-Street
and there were others,
Where the parish church ordained
An Anker, of faith - true.
An Anker in the Anker's house.

Two believers there resided.
Who wished to be ordained.
Percival and Cresacre they were named.
But one would be cheated of their aim.
An Anker in the Anker's house.

St Cuthbert with religious attributes many.
Women as Ankers, would not have any.
His dislike of women not known by many.
Women Ankers at Chester-le-Street there were never any.
An Anker in the Anker's house.

So it was.
That Percival Bowman as Anker was ordained.
With a service similar to burial rights,
Entombed to live, for many days and nights.
An Anker in the Anker's house.

So there he was, in dress so drab and humble.
In two rooms, one atop the other, so humble.
Through a small curtained church connection,
All his needs were passed.
An Anker in the Anker's house.

His only view of life, for life.
Through a small squint into the church.
Giving spiritual advice - so important.
Listening to worshippers' private problems.
An Anker in the Anker's house.

Even though an austere and comfortless life.
Prayer and contemplation, were his life.
Religion being for both giver and taker.
He began to think, more and more, of Anne Cresacre.
An Anker in the Anker's house.

After the Reformation, this way of life ended.
His life was changed, by another devotion sacred.
The ceremony, about a giver and a taker.
This house he left and wed Anne Cresacre.
An anchor no longer in the Anker's house.

A Sound Scientific Explanation Or Two

Soft silent silence sound.
Low pressure destroying.
High pressure shrieking.
Equilibrium seeking.
Only a wanton wilful wind.

Different atomic vibrations.
Different aural perceptions.
Oilrig divers' deceptions.
Helium causing voice alterations.
Only a voice emasculating gas.

Modern massive microwave measuring saucers
Interfering with outer space.
Neighbours interfering.
Cutting calm.
Only a musical megablaster.

Sound animated dancers
Wearing over-well-washed jeans.
Sound intelligence,
Intents and health.
Only a matter of genes.

Igneous Intrusions Into Boredom

Vertical cliffs showing strata seams
Seems all anticlinal and synclinal
So wavy!

Blocks protruding upwards intrude into the state of sea
Bounded by the sea's splashed boundary
So wearing!

Protrusions rough and jagged affect the state of the sea
Such forms wear to sea-smooth pebbles shiny,
The protrusions father the sea-smoothed sand.

The everlasting ebb and flow of tide and wave on pebbles
Mixing the pebbles with sandy beach
So time-weary! So wavy!

Seagulls stand on rocks
Lighthouses used to be built on rocks
Men mostly beware of rocks.

Rocks rarely moving can be boring
Boring and grading of rocks by man
So lucratively boring!

Men without wearying defend their rocks
The wearying blood-bought boundary of their state
Without wearing, unwearyingly proud.
So wearing!

It's The Waiting

It's the waiting
for what one knows what.

It's the waiting
for dawn's ending long night.

It's the waiting
for the season's lawn mowing's end.

It's the waiting
for the end of long winter's nights.

It's the waiting
for the end of wine's dreaming need.

It's the waiting
for loving wife's choice dress choice.

It's the waiting
for one's loved one's needful return.

It's the waiting
for a life success to provide all the answers.

It's the waiting for someone to care.

It's the waiting
for mother's baby's birth release.

It's the waiting. It's the waiting. It's the waiting
for the feeling that all's been worthwhile.

Thoughtful Acrostic

K indness of thought and action,
E ven when repeated
N ever palls
N ever palls.
E xpectations of one's future
T end to dull one's actions.
H ad the past been all worthwhile

G iven the gift of retrospection?
E ver vigilant
O ver-confident
R evel in your present youth.
G rievances remember, always expect an
E ar.

W ending one's life's way,
O verlooking its end
O verlooking its end
D eepens one's deeds
S tops the boredom.

Untitled

(Apologies to the mentors of:
Form (The Design and Craft of Writing) Course,
University of Durham - February to May 1998)

Student writers so still so still.
History of *Form* as yet unlearned.
Second summative unfinished still.

Anglo-Saxon French Italian *Form* fulfil.
Other poetry rhymed and metred.
Student writers so still so still.

Design the novel ambition fulfil.
18th century letter novels studied.
Second summative unfinished still.

Wish could compose a quick quadrille.
Now like Joyce's writing fractured.
Student writers so still so still.

Stream of consciousness will now distil.
Collage of oddments now fragmented.
Second summative unfinished still.

Mentors with style give hopes a will.
Writing now to be designed and crafted.
Student writers so still so still.
Second summative unfinished still.

A Parallel Poem About A Priest

Priest	*Christ*
Fairly fat and dressed in black.	Blood-crumpled cloth with
Hat sitting happily on a jovial face.	Crowned thorned agony.
Twinkling blue eyes smiled.	Tear-soaked eyes mild . . .
Ferociously religious but manner beguiled	God! This agony!
Sitting in the corner with his half of Mild	Thrust cloth't vinegar not
Priestly listening to our beery bawdry.	Joyous but jeery.
Now and again leading only rarely	Moaning appealing
With Irish Catholic just jokey story.	Forsaken me.

A Third Officer's Watch

N ow the moon shone.

I nterspersed with white shining clouds

G oing gracefully across moon's surface.

H oping for the coming dawn.

T hird officer of the watch

D oes end-of-watch duties.

A vast abaft and away.

Y earning and yawning.

´47 Photo Find

Four stand
at the house brick front.
Ages frozen
14 to 21.

Three stand
about the same height.
Youngest about
five inches slight.

All stand easy.
Hands front clasped,
back clasped,
free!

One jacket buttoned.
One by top button only.
With two jackets
untidily undone.

Three pullover and shirt-tied.
Lone one only
dull scarf patterned,
under jacket cross-battened.

Glancing at faces, faces glance
nothing there of importance.
Middle, side, non-parted hair.
One with battered Trilby on.

Brothers on left and right
now gone into the night.
Left inner left.
Right inner left . . . right!

Scillonian III

Early hotel breakfast with wide window view.
Early yacht outs through the harbour entrance reserve.
Awakens rested sea smooth surface
before its high tide retreat starts.

Now busily butting its way onwards.
Trailing with it its seagulls
their legs aerodynamically hidden.
Collecting scraps passenger seawards thrown.

Sick stirring swell begins to strike.
Passengers assert perfunctory prevention.
Is the seascape moving
in tune with the ships motion?

Island landing eventually made.
Sunny island flowers' beauty displayed.
Old man's sparse head hair area displayed.
Prevention liberally made with sun lotion's aid.

Holiday Journey

Early morning rise
for summer holiday start.
Seven nights away.

Suitcases crammed tight.
Three plastic boxes with
sandwiches of eggs and celery, a bite.

Towards Penzance by rail.
Through countryside and city
we resolutely race.

At Derby a rest
cold grey with rain.
Decided not to bring our macs again.

Many's the sandwich
have eaten thus far.
Intercom announcing, opening bar.

Glenys Moses

I am now a senior citizen, living on my own since the death of my husband. I lead an active life, go to church regularly, join my friends at our local Darby and Joan Club and still enjoy bowling, being a member of the Brecon Bowls Club.

My late husband and I were farming in this area for many years and that is why I enjoy writing poetry, I love the countryside and feel I have a special insight into what the countryside means to man and beast.

I have two sons, four grandsons and several grandchildren and six great grandchildren, which means I have a full and happy life.

The Sower

He grasps the small seed in a gnarled worn hand,
It falls without sound on the furrowed ground,
He walks along with a purposeful stride,
Confident, knowing the Lord will provide.
The faith is within, there's never a doubt
With moisture and warmth the seed will soon sprout.
Such is the harvest the soul can regain
Feeling the joy which can wipe out all pain.
Sowers can profit from seeds they have sown -
Biblical stories through ages passed down.
Worthwhile the effort, the harvest is great
Rewarding belief in God's holy state.
The sower is blessed with pride in his skill,
Perfect conditions with no thought of ill.
Proud of his prowess in spreading the word,
The harvest won't falter when prayers are heard.
He honours His promise, the crops will provide
Succour and comfort for man to survive.
Life is the pasture, we nurture it well -
Spreading good tidings and feeling the swell
Of deeds which then blossom with joy in the heart -
As Spring triggers movement and there is new start.

Trees

What do the trees say to my soul?
The solemn yew gives comfort
And calms the beating of my heart,
She enfolds babies in her arms -
Her love abounds.

The strong and silent oak stands firm,
Home of many a squirrel's drey,
Your gnarled frame greatly admired,
Your smooth timber crafted by man -
Living forever.

The hazel tree of smaller frame
Dances with catkins every spring,
And then in autumn the children come running
To pick up the sweet nuts,
Oh, happy hours.

Dark green holly with prickly leaves
Despised through the summer months -
But then through winter's darkest days
Your scarlet berries cheer the world -
And crown Christmas.

Memories

Memories are always special
And although they sometimes fade -
When brought back they give much pleasure -
And our dreams from them are made.
When as children, what enjoyment
When our birthdays came along,
Loving parents always guiding,
Bonds that are forever strong.
There are memories that sadden
Kept in corners of our hearts,
Wrapped away and seldom opened
For they make the teardrops start.
Special memories of milestones
When achievement came our way -
Giving life a concrete purpose
As we laboured every day.
In retirement we are happy -
Living at a slower pace,
Looking back with fondest memories
That our lives will always grace.
Friends we've met along life's highway
In our memories will stay,
Their encouragement and counsel
Helped us through the darkest day.
Memories, that special bonus
Giving joy as life goes on -
Fill the heart with golden moments,
For the bonds are sweet and strong.

Life

The sweet and happy memories linger on,
What joy they bring when years are rolling by,
Sweet youth's elixir was like honey gleaned
And stored forever in a haze of dreams.
No time to puzzle or from joy be weaned,
The memories washed away in bubbling streams.
And now as life slows down we stop and think,
There is no going back, the anchors hold,
We've lived our lives, and we are on the brink,
Ambition sleeps, and now we are not bold.
The joy of resting makes a perfect balm,
The lessons learned all give us inner calm.

Beauty

Beauty surrounds us as we make our way,
Gifts in abundance that brighten each day,
Flowers resplendent in glorious bloom
- Scented, and perfect, they drive away gloom.
Purple-topped mountains in powerful stance,
Vibrant perfection worth more than a glance.
Cascading waterfalls, sparkling and cold -
Far more exquisite than nuggets of gold.
Paintings enrapture, appeal to the eye,
Heartfelt emotion in baby's first cry.
Vistas of promise in fields that are green,
Paradise found in a fairy-tale scene.
All things of beauty enrapture the heart,
Midsummer glory when day makes its start.
Masterful music is beauty in sound,
Cherish the grandeur wherever it's found.
Beauty in nature as white snowflakes fall,
Christmastime fantasy all can recall.
Frost-patterned windows, so cold to the touch,
Past times of pleasure we loved very much.
Beauty in movement with birds on the wing,
Spellbound we listen as nightingales sing.
Colourful rainbows adorning the sky
Disappear quickly when rain has passed by.
Beauty in words that are honest and kind -
Rich in the power to stir heart and mind.
Beauty, the portion for which we all crave
Found in the chapters of birth to the grave.

Troubled Days

Who will bravely tackle all the ills we face -
Choking out the lifeblood of the human race?
Life has many problems, world-wide and at home,
Nightmares are emerging everywhere we roam.
Our forefathers struggled, sometimes life was sad
But they valued highly all the things they had.
They toiled endless hours, fighting for their bread,
Sundays then were sacred and the good word spread.
Now the world is greedy, standards slipped downhill,
Shameful is the pattern when man stoops to kill.
There are those who struggle, trying to impede
Vicious thugs and robbers who are ruled by greed.
Discipline has crumbled, what will be the end?
We must now take action and reverse the trend.
Governments must firmly strict new rules apply
For without such action our good land will die.
Value our past record, we must all unite
For with combined effort we can win the fight.
Count our many blessings and be very bold -
Let past values matter - they are framed in gold.

My Woodpile

There's a robin in my woodpile
Sitting on her nest so neat,
Made from grass and downy feathers -
Tireless work till it's complete.
Soon will hatch the tiny fledglings
Hidden well from prying eyes,
In a short while they'll be flying
And their home will be the skies.
There's a hedgehog in my woodpile,
Rolled up snugly in the leaves,
There he sleeps all through the winter -
Thankful for the warmth he feels
Many think a woodpile's boring,
Trunks and branches cast aside -
But in mine there's much excitement -
Keeping record gives me pride.
Children play around my woodpile
And their laughter fills the air,
Hide and seek and catch the beanbag
Are the games that they all share.
Landing on my woodpile branches
Butterflies of lovely hue,
Insects, moths, and once a grass snake
Slithered silently from view.
On the topmost branch, a blackbird
Often sings his morning song -
And a field mouse darts to cover
Hiding in the grasses long.
Every day there's something different,
Things that others do not see,
There's much life in my old woodpile
Bringing lots of joy to me.

Shadows

Shadows can be frightening, ominous and grey
And they bring depression on the darkest day.
Children hate the shadows, view them with dismay,
They are often frightened and their fear display.
When submerged by problems and we cannot cope -
Looking for the sunshine stirs an inner hope.
Shadows sometimes haunt you when you're feeling low,
Lift your guard up higher, stop the body blow.
Some have lived through shadows, battling through the years
Maybe wasting hours shedding bitter tears.
Why should shadows frighten? - they cannot attack,
Banish them with courage and they won't come back.
We need strength to conquer and a will of steel,
Only concrete effort will the problem heal.
We are all much happier when we see and know,
Feeling dark depression is a bitter blow.
There is no surrender, we must do or die,
Pity all the losers who sit down and cry.
Winning vicious battles fills the soul with pride,
Shadows are so futile, cast them all aside.
Scarred by life's tough battles, we can now reveal
How we overcame them, and what joy we feel.
Shining through the shadows came the sunlight's gleam,
New adventures prospered, we achieved our dream.
Those who win are honoured and success is great,
Pride in being a winner seals a happy fate.

Hope

Hope must be strong and never cast aside,
Bereft of hope, then life has lost all joy,
The will to live and walk with steadfast pride
Can urge us on, and willing hands employ.
Through every bitter trough of deep despair
We lean on those we love with anxious cry,
A gleam of hope in knowing they are there,
And deeper feelings glow with spirits high.
To all outsiders show a side that's strong -
Being wary of the pitfalls that appear.
Promote a strong belief where you belong,
Encourage others, be that listening ear.
Be brave in hope, there is no other way
A glorious dawning to another day.

Water

Crystal-clear, flowing, sparkling,
Vital gift bestowed on man,
Earth could not exist without it -
Part of God's own perfect plan.
Ships can sail across the ocean
Bringing goods the countries need,
Parched lands once again abundant -
With ability to feed.
Mountain streamlets cascade downwards
Swelling rivers as they flow,
Pastures in the valley flourish
As the luscious grasses grow.
Water, precious to the millions
Who enjoy its plenteous flow -
Piped into the towns and cities -
And the need will ever grow.
Water, what a wondrous asset,
In our thanks we offer praise -
Given to us in abundance -
Health and strength for all our days.

Music

Uplifted by the blend of perfect sound,
We search for it and find it everywhere,
Transported to a plane where joy is found,
Intense, and sweetly pleasing to the ear.
Music is found in nature's wild expanse -
The bubbling stream, the rushing of the sea,
The rustling of the trees where flowers dance,
The singing of the birds, the droning of the bee.
Music can stir a passion, then recede -
And quiet lullabies respond in dreams,
The rapture of the orchestra can lead
To pinnacles ecstatic and supreme.
Composers earn reward from hours spent,
With music we can live in sweet content.

John Ramsden

My name is John Ramsden. I am a retired entertainer/compare and I have been writing poetry for a number of years on various subjects. I began by writing comic profiles for friends on their birthdays and then progressed to poems, odes and rhymes. In my younger days I produced and directed a charity concert party performing in various venues around the district raising funds for local charities.

During my years of writing I have had several pieces of my work published in anthologies and in 1996 I received an Award of Excellence from Poetry in Print, National Open Poetry Competition of which I am proud. I get great satisfaction from hearing that my work has been approved by my family and friends, more so when praise comes from publishers who have accepted my work.

Most of my poems are written on a whim, such as hearing the birds singing in my garden or the moon shining through the window, even a flower growing in the garden. I write lots of dedications in rhyme on various subjects such as the local fire fighters, local heroes and many more. I also have written a few short stories and my interest in music prompted me to write a song (words and music) on the occasion of my late mother's 80th birthday and on the birth of my first grandchild. I also like to paint in oils and water-colours. I enjoy cooking and baking as I trained as a cook whilst serving my National Service in 1954/56.

I have been married for 47 years and have 3 sons and 2 daughters and have been retired for 3 years, during which time I have written almost 200 poems, odes and rhymes and I hope to continue writing for a great many more years.

In Safe Hands

I often wonder how we cope
Especially when there's no hope
Of travelling back to long past years
And leaving behind our present-day fears
So face them we must and be quite brave
If our sanity we want to save
Face the world and bear the cross
Thinking not about the loss
We must hold our heads up with great pride
Take the future in our stride
And hope that others will show no remorse
And just let nature take its course
That's the way that we must cope
And never, never give up hope.

All In A Day's Work

Morning mist like an eerie cape
Over fields of yellow rape
Farm gate swinging in the breeze
New leaves forming on the trees
Cattle calling, 'It's milking time'
Walk the lane of mud and grime
Hens that flutter trying to fly
Cat approaching from nearby
Sheepdog sleeps throughout it all
Barn owl hooting, hear his call
Barn door open, stacked with hay
Fodder for a winter's day
Plough horse peering over the stable door
Logs stacked neatly by the door
Cart shaft broken, can't be wheeled
Sheep roam freely in the field
Fast approaching the month of May
For the farmer, just another day.

Wasted Years

When people ask, 'Are you in love?'
I look up to the sky above
And think of all the wasted years
And the times that I have hidden from my fears
Fears of ending on my own and spending all my life alone
But until the right girl comes along
I'll hide my emotions in a song

When friends ask, 'When will you learn?'
And show me of their true concern
I'll be content to sit and wait
Hoping that it's not too late
I've tried before without success
My life has always been a mess
So until I find where I went wrong
I'll hide my emotions in a song

I tell myself that the day will come
When I can say to everyone,
'I've met the sweetheart of whom I've dreamed'
Now nothing's as bad as it first seemed
The light of love shines in our eyes
True love I've come to recognise
So now I'll tell the world of my love so strong
And sing my emotions in a song.

The Garden

Evening sunlight shining bright
Through the window, a wonderful sight
Pretty flowers nodding their heads
A gentle breeze skirts their beds
Evergreens shine with emerald glow
Lupins, roses and poppies grow
In the rockery, alpines flourished
All well-watered, all well-nourished
Through the window a summer scene
The garden is peaceful, so serene
Birds do sing and white doves coo
Butterflies and bees all summer through
In the tall trees the birds do nest
Summer evenings at their best
When sunlight fades and night draws in
Light will lose and dark will win.

Dawn

Dawn is breaking, come the light
Gone the darkness of the night
Birds are singing in the trees
Branches swaying in the breeze
Shadows forming on the ground
Flowers awakening all around
Grass still damp with morning dew
Reflecting a sky of pastel blue
Cotton wool clouds float way up high
Signs are showing spring is nigh
Night owl safely in his nest
Sleeping through a day of rest
Foxes return to their lair
Wild geese soar through the air
Soon the town will come alive
All is well, we will survive
Doves are cooing, hear their call
A brand new day is born for all.

Seasons

Springtime brings the flowers in May
Fast gone Easter, now holiday
Summer sun in warm July
Kissed the month of June goodbye
Autumn turns the leaves to gold
Nights now shorter, turning cold
Winter days when snowflakes fall
December time for Santa's call
Before we know it, it's New Year's Eve
Then spring again, would you believe?

Daffodils and tulips make a spring
Grass is greener, birds now sing
Longer nights mean summer is here
Sunshine days are everywhere
Autumn leaves from tall trees fall
Tawny owls begin to call
Wintertime comes round again
Snowflakes settle in the lane
Before we know it, it's New Year's Eve
Then spring again, would you believe?

One Whole Year

January starts a brand new year
Far away from Christmas cheer
February dark and colder
Everything one month older
March brings spring with buds and flowers
April with it brings rain showers
May a month of festive dance
Of the summer just a glance
June begins our summertime
Holidays and all things fine
July days of sunshine bright
Early dawn and longer night
August comes with many weathers
Sunshine, rain and perfumed heathers
September when the nights draw in
Threatening signs of winter begin
October shorter days are here
Fog and mist will soon appear
November may bring winter snow
Thoughts of Christmas and mistletoe
December here it's Christmastime
Sleigh bells, carols and pantomime
Every year is twelve months long.
Don't look now, one's just gone!

That Face

I saw your face amongst the crowd
I felt that I should call out loud
You hadn't changed, you looked the same
If only I could remember your name
You looked so smart, so chic and cool
I saw you first whilst at school
You were the favourite of all the boys
As they stood admiring your poise
Tall and slender, pretty and yet
You were never the teacher's pet
If only I could find the nerve
To give you the greeting that you deserve
I would come over but I'm too shy
You walked towards me but passed right by.

Dilemma

I went to find a tissue to blow my nose upon
But when I reached out for the box I found there wasn't one
I walked into the bathroom to get some toilet paper
I couldn't see just where it was the room was full of vapour
I groped and groped and felt around for something to blow in
But in the mist I couldn't see just where I was going
I found a towel on the bath but it was wet beyond belief
So I decided there and then to use my handkerchief
If it wasn't for that, Heaven knows!
I could still be chasing a running nose
Who knows?

Lost And Found

Yes, he has surely lost it and doesn't seem to care
All he ever does all day is sit there in his chair
I have never seen him smiling or break into a grin
He is always seen with his top lip resting on his chin
I don't think he ever had one I've never seen it used
For if he ever did so his face would be confused
So read a little further and you may get to know
What it is that he has lost, the mournful so-and-so
But if we all are patient he may put on a show
Then on his face without disgrace a smile may grow
What he has lost is something that everyone must possess
To help and keep us happy and sane no less
Oh no, don't look now, that frown is back again
It really looks as if his face is full of pain
I have never seen a laughter line around his sad grey eyes
He always looks so forlorn and that is no surprise
What it will take to make him laugh we may never know
But if I see the sign of a smile I will tell you so
And should his top lip move from off his chin
He may then surprise us with a grin
Perhaps his mind will tell his brain
That it's now time to smile again
If it does I'll tell the world there is no truth in the rumour
That the man sat here has found his sense of humour.

Days Gone By

Just an old-fashioned street
Where us kids used to meet
We'd skip and we'd hop
And play whip and top
Marbles in the gutter, kick ball fly
Paper chase, bouncy ball high
A game of rounders we would sneak
Skipping ropes and hide and seek
Didn't want to be the first look-out
Making sure the beat bobby wasn't about
Hand stand-ups against the wall
Who will be the first to fall?
Cartwheel acrobats in the road
But we all knew the Highway Code
A game of 'tiggy', the odd road race
Everything at a steady pace
We would play from dusk till dawn
'Til our poor old feet were worn
Cowboys and Indians, perhaps a war game
Things will never again be the same
The war now ended, it's peace again
I've enjoyed my walk down Memory Lane
Now the months and years unfold
I suppose it's me, I'm growing old!

Heartache And Pain

I need to tell you now and tell you the truth
I really do love you and I'll show you the proof
I promise to love you as long as I live
We need to be together, we've so much love to give
It's time to remember all the good things that we had
Reflecting on the best times and forgetting the bad
Won't you listen to your heart, let's go right back to the start
We can learn to love again and end my suffering and pain
I will make you happy and show how much I care
I want you there beside me, I need to know you're there
I need to feel your closeness and hold you once again
Each lonely night without you brings back all the pain
Please listen to your heart, dear, let's go back to the start
We can fall in love again and mend my broken heart.

Tranquillity

Come sail with me across a tranquil sea
Come sail to my special island
With gold moonbeams and silver streams
Where dreams come true and troubles fade
Where we can keep the promises we made
Here on my special island, my island of dreams
Where shining seas lap golden sand
Where we as lovers strolled hand in hand
Beneath a cloudless sky and that is why
You must sail with me to my special island
My island of dreams
Where promises are not just words
And nothing is as it seems
And true love lasts forever and lovers
Share their dreams
Where peace and love and happiness reign side by side
We'll let all our emotions be our faithful guide
If only you will sail with me to my special island
My island of real dreams.

Summer Outing

We are going on a charabanc ride
Spending the day at the seaside
With golden sand and a clear blue sky
In crystal water where ships sail by
Where children play on sandy dunes
And hurdy-gurdies play a tune
The helter-skelter towers high
And a roller coaster, my oh my!
Buckets and spades are at the ready
To build a sandcastle firm and steady
With a little flag to flutter in the breeze
Mum and Dad on bended knees
Digging real deep to build a moat
Grandma lying on her coat
Grandad lazing in a deckchair
A happy family gathered there
No more complaining about his gout
Just enjoying a good day out
Picnic basket full of eats
Small ham sandwiches, fruit and sweets
Orange juice and lemonade
A flask of tea, we've got it made
Seagulls flying and a rising tide
Happy day at the seaside.

Christmas

Christmas trees, holly and mistletoe
Icicles, robins and pure white snow
Carollers singing and church bells ring
Sleighs and Santa Claus, what joy they bring
Fairy lights, starry nights with Jack Frost here
Christmas crackers and red-nosed deer
Snowmen standing in the yards
Postman bringing Christmas cards
Children sleeping safe and sound
Dreaming of the morning I'll be bound
All these things are on display
Ready and waiting for Christmas Day.

Sara Campbell-Kelly

I am 21 years old and come from Macclesfield, Cheshire. I've been living in Reading, Berkshire for the past three years whilst at university. I am currently in my fourth and final year of a Fine Art degree.

I have always loved the English language and have what you might call, an obsession with words and their limitless possibilities. I started writing in my early teens whilst I was going through a particularly hard time in my life. I found it easier to express myself in verse so my early work is very personal and more like a diary. As time went on and I became happier in life, I also grew more confident in my writing style and progressed into exploring a broader range of subjects. My work always stems from personal life experience and I do still use it as a diary to work out problems or thoughts, or simply to record events.

I have many influences including writers such as Maya Angelou (in particular, her poem 'Still I Rise') Brian Patten and Benjamin Zephaniah. I also draw from a diverse selection of artists and musicians, such as Mark Quinn, Hayley Newmann, Bruce Naumann, Tori Amos, Tool and India Arie. I love lyrically rich performers and art that touches me in some way, there are far too many to mention! My poems focus on subjects like love, contemplation and realisation. I try to inject them with optimism, as this is a large part of my character.

See

The end of the world's expanse.
Miles taken
All in a glance,
With photographic eyes.
Desperate waves,
Mirrored in the sky.

I'm surfing,
Empowered on the shore.
Riding white horses
In my top hat and tails,
With my back straight
And my soul in the air.
Feeling omnipotent as God,
Looking as far
As the eye can see.

Shiver

I'm trying to warm myself,
By curling up in your
Wispy clouds.

You're talking at me,
Hot in my ear.
Whilst I watch the sky
And feel the weather change.

My shivers come,
Cos I never know
What you mean to say,
Amongst all those words
And affectionate terms,
Used for me and all
The other girls.

Mantra

We're treading on time
With illusions of wealth.
We're being crept upon
With stealth.

Sometimes you
Forget to live,
And crawl
Head down,
With body stiff.

Sometimes you
Breathe me in,
Nestled inside hair
And breast.
Inhaling jokes
And pieces of hope,
As each second
Spills out life.

I thought you could use
A song to dance to.
Feel how its heart beats.
Listen to this mantra,
Won't you?

Dream

I've been with you
All night, across
Our south to north
Divide. You're almost
Touchable in sleep.
So real.

This morning,
I'm alone;
But held, content.
If I move one hair
This cocoon will break.
I feel the pillow,
As if you, curled
Inside my shape.

I was woken by
Your phone call
- You were with me.
Our muddy-eyed
Morning talk
Blessed my day.
And then we did it
All again.

Stand Slow

I know I've got to stand slowly,
To let an image of me grow
In the minds of
My chosen spectators.
But I want to jump up
And divulge all, now!

There are some things
Only few know;
Things I tell
When the storm blows.

My door is swinging
In the wind.
Banging shut,
I'm breathing as it opens.
Quietly protected,
I'm periodically exposed.

Transported

This night is fine
Sat on the step,
Of our empty house.
I'm spread thinly,
So it's nice to have
Some time for myself.

Live jazz is drifting
In the air,
Sent from the pub
Across the road,
With love.

Duke Ellington and I
Are sipping cheap vodka
And Coke; we're away!

The night dreams on
And I'm encapsulated.
Exhausting myself
With excitement, dancing
Loudly in my silent nod.

This is a drug, seldom used,
But loved! I remember now,
This music is urging me
To play.

I'd love to pick up
Where I left off,
And take a ride again.
Carried by a smiling,
Warming, hiding feeling.

My saxophone, the catalyst
Of what I can never describe;
The ride.
This evening's holiday
Is welcome.

Absorbed by every
Breezy note,
I'm flying on all
Memories and hopes,
As they duck
And soar
And dive
And coast . . .

Sick

His sickness
Became her disease.

She swallowed all he fed her,
Licking crumbs off the knife.
Taking only the sharpest
From her double-edged life.

Staring at her empty plate,
She was lonely;
Infected with hate.
Not for him, but
Only for herself.

He'd jailed her soul
And turned the key.
She erected steel bars,
With an iron heart,
Made silently.

She feels sometimes
I've been naïve,
To believe that she
Could ever be free.

Though, I know
It's possible, cos
The angels rescued me.
When his sickness
Became my disease,
The only thing to keep
Was faith.

At Angel

Pint of Fosters at Angel.
Toilets downstairs.
I've fixed my hair,
Suits me.

Darkness through the window,
It's raining tonight.
Distorted views and
Heavy clouded skies.

The couple opposite me,
White wine chat,
At Angel.
I'm the only one
Without company.

I'm quite enjoying it;
All dance and no regret.
This is my loneliness,
Documented and meant.

Solitude, attitude.
I haven't written about
What has struck me the most
At all.

Fruit

I'm watching the birds on the lake,
As they travel along their moving
Ripples of light and dark.
Sitting in front of the sun
With the wind blowing on my back.
I was never the same after you had gone,
But not because of anything I lacked.

The birds all fly together,
Never leaving friends behind.
They're circling the water,
Then all at once they dive.

Without you, I wouldn't
Have become who I am.
I found love in the palm of your hand.
It was a fragile kind of love,
But I clung to it;
Sucking on its juice,
Whilst you squeezed it like
A tender fruit in your fist.

I was still sucking
Long after the decay occurred,
Because you added to my life
And I missed you in my world.

Sunday Washing

I lay in bed all morning,
Hearing the washing machine
Through my bedroom floor.
But connected to my mum,
Via Radio Four.

I stared at the cobwebs
In each corner of my room,
Wondering how on earth
They got there. Before
Dusting them away
With a clean tissue.

Then, I washed my hair and my heart,
Whilst standing in our
Leaky bath this afternoon.

I'm doing some Sunday washing.
I'm not in church,
But I'm cleansing my
Clothes and myself.
A day of quiet.
Subconscious reflection
Of the week that's past.

Nightlife

Lying here with my headphones on.
I'm alone.
It's the middle of the night
and my thoughts are playing
full blast.

I'm thinking of nothing,
which seems everything,
when the lyrics start to sculpt.
My cheeks are burning,
but my feet are still cold

The house is quiet
whilst I'm in this room,
lying in my world.
Stories run from their middle
to beginning and I'm
making up the end.

My wandering mind is sluggish,
but still buzzing.
Cos this song has reminded
me of you.

Golden

She asked me a question
and my heartbeat picked up pace.

She didn't like my silence
but I said it with a smile on my face.

Past Living

His mind rests on hot coals
Not seeming to care,
Sleeping through the days
And waking in the past,
With the future blurring by.

He's woken;

By slices of reality.
His daydreams are broken,
He recalls no serenity.
He's missed his future,
His time in the present,
The time of his life.

Lost

You dance without a care
- I watch. Mutual escapism.
Your smile enhances this
paradise room and as my heart
falls into your pillow lips, it
smiles and strangely morphs.

Your sweet taste excites me
and I feel warm within your
unfamiliarity. We pull away
from our introduction and
I realise I've found myself,
lost through your eyes.

We travelled like this,
Brown and deep.
I was never lost again; until
someone moved the signposts.

Presently, I'm unravelling
a ball of wool. Connected
to your memory.
Walking . . .

Jo Stimpson

 I was born in Newport, Shropshire in 1943. At present I live in Stoke-on-Trent with my partner and husband of eighteen years. Although he is not a poetry reader as such, my husband encourages me to pursue an ambition of mine, that is to have my poems recognised.

As a mother of six children, I have many memories of their childhood, writing them bedtime stories, days out at the seaside etc.

Now that I have grandchildren I compare their young lives with those of my own children and also my own childhood. How things have changed! I grew up in the country and on a return to the village where I was born I was disappointed at what I saw; the changes to such a small village were unbelievable!

Now that I am retired, I have more time to concentrate on writing poetry. When people read my poems I hope they will be able to cast their minds back and remember similar events that happened to them such as moving house, revisiting places they once loved, their first grandchild, missing a loved one, all the things that mean so much in so many different ways, maybe this will bring a smile as they remember.

I find inspiration in things around me, especially this time of year, the children's Christmas Eve rituals; at the same thinking what is it really all about, the changes that affect all our lives and what they mean to us.

Christmas Eve

It's Christmas Eve today
Santa and his reindeer will be coming my way
I've hung up my stocking and said my goodnights
I'll climb into bed and put out the lights
I've been very good and kind you know
I do hope Santa will get through the snow
There's lots of mince pies for him to eat
A nice warm fire for his poor old feet
Milk for the reindeer, just by the door
I was just too tired, to do anymore.

Christmas morning is here, oh gee!
Just look at the presents under the tree
There's lots of goodies to drink and eat
Nanas and Grandads to hug and greet

Now it's the end of my exciting day
Thank you Santa for coming my way
As I wearily climb up the stairs
I must not forget to say my prayers
'God bless Mummy and Daddy too
And God bless baby Jesus, we all love you.'

Just For You

Our house was neat and tidy, very quiet too
Then we found out, Mummy was having you
There are tests to be done, and then a scan
Such excitement, I'm going to be a gran
Knitting needles clicking, with wools of white and blue
The nursery's nearly ready, just for you
Grandad's in his den planning and scheming
Or is he just sitting there quietly dreaming
Of things that Grandads and little boys do?
He's planning something, just for you

Then you arrive, weighing six pounds three
Daddy looks on proudly, while Mummy drinks her tea
You have tiny little fingers, tiny little toes
Lots of hair and the cutest nose
Lying in your cradle fast asleep
Photos are taken to treasure and keep.

Going out is 'neat and tidy' and all the quietness too
Coming in are toys, noise and the joy of you!

What Are Girls Made Of?

Girls are made of sugar and spice,
When I look at you, I have to think twice
Your untidy hair is all over the place
You rollerblade at a terrible pace
Shouting and yelling at the boys next door
Leaving your clothes all over the floor
You keep bugs in jars out in the shed
Conkers and marbles under your bed
Daughters are pretty, sweet and clean
Well, that was the girl I saw in my dream
Although you have brought me so much joy
I'm sure you should have been a boy

Then you started secondary school
You acted peculiar, you called it 'cool'
Now forgotten are your bugs in the shed
You've tidied your room, even under the bed
Once again I'm in despair
I want to ask, but I don't dare
What has changed you in such a short time?
I ask, 'Are you ill?' You say you're fine
Your dad reckons you've been bitten by the love bug
Come here, give your mum a hug
You will always bring me joy
I'm so glad you're not a boy!

My Special Friend

You can make friends in all kinds of places
Good friends, true friends
Friends with kind and smiling faces

I had a friend who was all of these
He was gentle and kind, and so easy to please
If I was sad or feeling down
My special friend was always around
He'd look at me as if to say
'Let's go for a walk, it'll be OK'
We've walked in the sun, the rain and snow
And all my troubles seemed to go

You were treasured right from the start
The day you died, it broke my heart
I'll never forget our walks in the rain, sun and snow
My doggy friend, I miss you so.

What Is Love?

What is love? I don't know
If you catch it, does it show?
Is it the welcome home kiss, when you've been away
Or the sunshine, on an autumn day?
An open fire making toast
Or just enjoying the things we like the most?

The joy of a bride, through a veil of lace
Or the first ever smile on a baby's face
Early snowdrops on a carpet of snow
Is this love? I don't know

Maybe it's all around
Flying in the sky, growing in the ground
In the simple words that children sing
Or the shiny gold of my wedding ring

Oh, you can catch it, yes, it's true
I caught love from all these things and 'you'.

I Wish I Could Go Back

A long time ago, when I was a child
There was a field by our house where flowers grew wild
Buttercups, daisies, violets, primroses
We had fun making daisy chains, and wild flower posies
In the field was a stream
It was every little fishing boy's dream
Armed with a jam jar and a butterfly net
The boys would see how many things they could get
Little minnows and tadpoles, were put in the jar
'We can come again tomorrow? It's not very far'

We went again the next day, for different things to see
There were rabbits playing in the grass, such a lovely sight to see
Water voles and little moles playing happily
I was just remembering days gone by
Kids don't do it nowadays, I often wonder why
I've grown up now and moved away
I wish I could go back there, just for the day.

Granny's Button Box

My granny had a button box, I remember it well
For each pretty button, there was a story to tell
There were buttons from blouses, jumpers and skirts
Even some from Grandad's old shirts
Granny never threw a button away
'One day, it may come in handy,' she'd say
Her buttons were her memories, of times good and bad
I'm glad she shared her memories of the life that she'd had
The button box is mine now, I still open it now and then
The memories of her stories keep flooding back again
No one will ever understand
Why I love this little box, I'm holding in my hand.

My Garden

In my garden I'd like to see
An array of colours looking at me
Roses, pansies, that kind of thing
Not bugs and slugs and nettles that sting
Maybe some fish in a little pond
Oh Fairy Godmother, I need your wand!

I've bought some tools, and things to sow
On with my wellies, and off I go
Watch out bugs, you'd better hide
The roses and pansies are on my side

Some time later, I can see
A patch of ground that is weed-free
I've sown some flowers and veggies too
But listen, bugs, I'm not through with you

There's a compost heap, behind the shed
Now off with you, there's your bed
Take your friends along with you
And vacate my garden, go on, shoo!

The DIY's Goffer

I'm a DIY's goffer, sad but true
I wouldn't do it for anyone else but you
A shelf needs making, I get the wood
I would do it myself, if only I could
I fetch the tape, then the nails
Next the hammer, then he wails
'Where's the level?'
'The level?' said I, 'is this a riddle?'
He then shows me this thing with a bubble in the middle
An explanation was given for 'the bubble'
Is it so important, all this trouble?
He says, 'If a job's worth doing, do it right.
It'll get done properly, if it takes all night'
Maybe next time I'll phone for a man, with a tool box in his van
But I would save money, goffering for my very own perfect DIY man.

Powder And Paint

Little pots of powder, little pots of paint
Makes Nana's complexion just what it ain't
How is it, whenever you call
I find Nana's miracles all over the wall?

There's lipstick flowers all over the floor
Eyeliner trees, painted on the door
The toilet roll is colourful too
With eye shadow of brown and blue

I bought you colouring books, and your own pots of paints
You see, my complexion needs to be what it ain't
So please little darling, use your own
And leave Nana's powders and paints alone.

Why Is It?

Why is it whenever I'm taking a bath
Going shopping, and I'm nearly down the path
The phone rings?
Unlock the door, pick up the receiver, politely say, 'Hello'
The call says, 'Did you know
We are selling double glazing at a very special rate?'
I say, 'I've had mine done so you're too late'

Do these callers know how angry I feel
When I sit down for my evening meal
The phone rings again
Selling something or other, it's such a pain
The most annoying thing of all
Whenever I make a telephone call
I am told 'Please hold,
You're in a queue, or we'll get back to you'

If I need double glazing, or Sky TV
I will make the appropriate telephone call
And invite you to visit me
Until then, please leave me alone
Otherwise I may not answer that dreaded phone.

Moving House

Moving house, what a pain
I'm never doing it again
Curtains don't fit, carpets don't fit
Oh where is the sense in it?

There are boxes piled up at the gate
Where's the van? He's running late
Oh the hassle, oh the strain
I'm never moving house again

Here's van in such a hurry
The driver says, 'I'm here love, don't you worry'
Three hours later everything in
The furniture, crockery, pedal bin

Finally we arrive at number eleven
Will this be my idea of Heaven?
Now at last, the key's in the door
There's unwanted mail all over the floor

Well, the carpets are down, the curtains are up
On with the kettle, we all need a cup
Where are the biscuits we bought for the brew?
I'm still not sure about this, are you?

One week later, and here we are
Everything's polished, even the car
Cupboards are tidy, everything's so clean
It's a little palace, fit for a queen
Oh, the hassle, oh the strain
I'm never moving house again.

What Happened To?

I took a trip down Memory Lane today,
Back to the village where I was born, and I have to say
I didn't like what I saw, everything's changed
The whole of the village, has been rearranged.

The little school I went to, when I was five
Used to be so busy and happy, so alive
Now it's a bungalow, no more children's chatter and noise
A man and wife live there now, with their two baby boys
The pub's still there, although that's changed too
It's a holiday inn now, the prices they charge, phew!

Gone are the fields I played in and tobogganed in the snow
Why did the lovely countryside have to go?
To make way for more houses and roads
What will happen to the hedgehogs and toads?
I watched animals like these when I was a child
Playing in the meadows, where buttercups grew wild.

How many more trees will have to come down
To make way for second homes for those from the town?
Will they ever appreciate how it used to be here
In the beautiful countryside, some of us hold dear?

Mother Said

Mother said, 'Eat lots of fruit and plenty of greens
You'll never have spots when you're in your teens.
If you eat all your crusts from off your bread
It will make your hair curly, on top of your head
Eat up your carrots, they will make your eyes bright
You'll be able to see in the dark at night
Always wear a vest to protect your back,
Vitamins A, B, C and D, you must not lack
In the winter wrap up warm, wear sensible shoes
Now do as you're told, when you're older you can choose'
I am older now, and I tell my children the same
I guess it's Mother by nature, Mother by name.

A Game From Yesterday

Come here, boys, and stand with me
Under the spreading chestnut tree
I used to stand like this, with your dad
It was a long time ago, when he was a lad

Little brown things falling to the ground
If you look in the grass, more can be found
'What are they, what do they do?'
'Let's take some home and I'll show you'

You're holding these things, so shiny and brown
You say, 'We don't have these where we live in our town'
'They're horse chestnuts, 'conkers' to me and you'
Then I explain whilst making holes for laces to go through
I show the boys how to play the game
School playtimes may never be the same again
'Hold onto your conker very tight
Now whack mine with all your might'
As I watched yours fall and sway
Mine lives to be whacked another day
Your dad calls to take you home, looks at your shoes and red faces
But just like then, Nana has 'spare laces'.

Ouch!

When you were a baby, 'ouch' meant teeth were coming through
You fell and bumped your head, 'ouch' that hurt too
At school, 'ouch' meant injections in your arm
Falling off your bike, 'ouch' but it's done no harm
Scrapes and grazes, pains in the tummy
Who's there with plasters and potions? 'Mummy'

A teenager's heart that's broken in two
This time plasters and potions won't do
You vow never to love again
Mum mops up tears, that fall like rain
She knows one day you'll change your mind
When it's time, true love you'll find
This time you'll marry, it will be for keeps
Now Mum doesn't mind when her little girl weeps.

Tales Of The Riverbank

The alarm went off at the crack of dawn
'Please excuse me if I yawn'
The car's packed up, we're off for the day
'Dress casual,' is all he would say
'Where are we going?' I wanted to know
'When will we get there, is it far to go?'
We drove off the road, down a beaten track
It's quite near home so I could go back
I won't spoil your day of fishing
Although it doesn't stop me wishing
If I was a child, I wouldn't find it so boring
Instead I would go exploring,
So I think I will . . .
As I roam through the brambles in the morning sun
How I remember, it was such fun
'The Tales of the Riverbank', all of them are true
I've seen where the moles live, and Ratty too
There's a hidden place where the badger built his sett
A tiny hole where the mouse lives, though I'haven't seen him yet
Mr Toad came out of his hall
Just as a squirrel came to call
I came fishing but, found it boring
It was much more fun to go exploring
Now I'm sitting here, on my fold-up chair
Enjoying the warmth of the evening air
Life on the riverbank begins slowing down
Dragonflies are cruising, instead of rushing up and down
The water hen takes her babies to the nest
They've been swimming all day, and need their rest
The fish have gone to sleep now, so you will catch no more
We're on our way home now, I've had a lovely day
Fishermen come and go but 'the tales of the riverbank' are here to stay.

Shadows

Shadows in the dark, all over the wall
When morning comes, they're not there at all
Where do they come from, where do they go?
Who makes them, does anybody know?
On my own in the dark, I have seen many things
Witches on broomsticks, and birds with large wings
Cute little bunnies with big floppy ears
Hobgoblins and demons and Indians with spears

Tomorrow will start another new day
All the shadows will have gone far away
Soon you'll be on your way home to me
Tonight the only shadow I'll see
Is your shadow through the glass in the door
No scary shadows anymore.

Ron Bissett

From my early school years I found a keen interest in writing and had once entertained the idea of becoming a professional journalist. This failed to materialise however, since my second aim of going to sea prevailed. A career in the Royal Navy, lasting twenty-two years, did provide me with a wealth of travel experience upon which to concentrate my creative writing. Time being limited, I found that writing poetry in rhyme, became a pleasant diversion.

Following my service career; two shorter periods in both local government and management; were followed by fifteen years as a sales representative, until retirement in 1996.

Since then, I have had more time to pursue my writing and been fortunate in having some 121 poems published to-date, in various anthologies. I would, however, like to produce volumes of my poems in the near future. I prefer the more traditional forms of verse, always in rhyme, since I neither like nor understand blank verse.

I intend to produce an autobiography eventually; at present this has been all but completed in rhyme. However, it is anticipated that I shall have to convert to prose, in order to fully accommodate my lifetime experiences.

Music in many forms, provides me both with relaxation and on occasion stimulation, for poetic works. I work best while listening to most types of music, which can on occasion became the catalyst for a poem.

If asked what my subjects or themes might be, I could only answer, 'About life and living,' as any true poet might agree. I greatly appreciate the talent of such poets as John Betjeman, Rudyard Kipling, John Masefield, Edgar Allen Poe, Robert Service and Thomas Gray. Apart from choosing interesting subjects, their ability to produce excellent rhythm and rhyme I always find very enjoyable and stimulating.

Capital Offence

He murdered your lover,
    And then he was found;
You longed for sweet vengeance;
    For justice profound!

When the police had arrested,
    Their suspect so strong;
By the evidence tested,
    They couldn't be wrong!

He was questioned with vigour,
    His answers were weak;
No way could he figure,
    The right way to speak!

Alibis and excuses,
    Were all proved untrue;
Detection deduces,
    They came from the blue!

Remand followed clearly,
    The court date was set;
So retribution nearly,
    You shortly would get!

The verdict awaited,
    By jury was brought;
The guilt had been stated,
    But what if it's not?

The judge donned the cap,
    Would the prisoner now hang?
No escape from the trap -
    Door, which closed with a bang!

So justice prevailed,
    Were they on the right track?
But what if they failed?
    They could not bring him back?

Communicative Instrument

A boon, necessity, or curse?
To be without, which would be worse?
It causes joy - or makes you moan,
Where would we be, without a phone?

Such joy, or anger, or regret,
With direct contact being met;
For solving problems, distance-wise,
Our phone's an angel, in disguise!

Disturbing, silence breaking noise!
Or welcoming, a long lost voice;
For bringing news, both bad and good,
Or being fully - understood!

Congrats! Condolences or joy;
Informing - was it girl or boy?
That vital game - what was the score?
Forgotten items, from the store!

In business, facts and figures pass,
Statistics all, we can amass!
One simple call, with such precision,
Can often make - the right decision!

Relating gossip, chasing blues!
Wit neighbours, friends, expressing views!
Cheering those, who are alone!
The perfect way - by telephone!

Inventions come - this one's the best!
By far surpassing all the rest;
For vocal contact, who can tell?
This patent held by A G Bell!

Deceptive Reasoning

Holding to conceptual notions,
      Being convinced of righteous ways;
Living with intense emotions,
      Devastates the best of days!

Beyond the pale of common sense,
      Where night brings no relief;
When little things - may seem immense,
      And logic - past belief!

If fear becomes the rational,
      And thinking is obscene;
Then what of the traditional?
      The things which might have been!

Bravely facing confrontation,
      Courage filling every nerve;
Challenging hallucination,
With degrees of sudden verve!

Within the grasp of understanding,
      Lies a world of disbelief;
As hidden by the brain's demanding,
      Solace, in its hour of grief!

Then living with imagination,
      Awakening the ripened state;
To the hour of provocation,
      Bowing to the hand of fate!

Felinus Typicalus

Feline, hunting in the night,
Seeking other cats to fight!
Knowing what you're missing;
Arching, clawing, hissing;
Birds and mice,
Are really nice!
But definitely, not the dog!
You terribly ferocious 'Mog'!

Feline, grooming by the fire,
Your outings always seem to tire!
Miaowing, scratching, purring;
Mealtimes then occurring;
Fish and meat,
With milk to follow - lapping!
And soon, we find you - napping!

Friends

Some we see most every day,
Others once a year;
Some live very far away,
Others live quite near.

Meeting brings us so much joy,
With such a lot to say;
Busily our minds employ,
Within their time of stay.

Hearing how their families are,
Their health - has it been good?
On holidays, have they been far?
Your interest - understood!

How have the kids been doing at school?
At work have things gone well?
Just making every minute full,
With much to hear and tell!

Remembered secrets bring a grin,
You can recall such fun;
Yet also many hopes you pin,
For dreams that have begun!

Then all too soon, it's time to leave,
Regretfully, their visits ends;
To meet again, you must believe,
They will remain good friends!

The Laptop!

I bought the wife a laptop,
I hoped she'd have some fun!
But then she kept me busy,
Seeing the things she'd done!

She opened up the Windows,
Then pressed the delete key!
She thought that it was broken!
And asked for help from me.

Again we got it working,
The manual must be read!
When next she had a problem,
She came to me instead!

Now I'm a desktop user,
And laptops ain't my scene.
It takes a little time then,
To see where she has been!

I try to maintain patience,
And keep her on the track;
But if she fills my day up,
I'll send that laptop - back!

Morning Musings

In Spring, sun barely up, it's morning,
Get out of bed, just half awake!
Before alarm can ring its warning,
Shiver with the shower you take!

In Summer, sun's been up for ages,
Mornings when it's bright and warm;
Then pleasant days begin in stages,
Everyone is in good form!

In Autumn, mornings start more slowly,
Clocks go back, the days are short;
Proceedings start with spirits lowly,
Feelings of the saddest sort!

In Winter, and the days begin much later,
Weather cold and dark instead;
You become a morning hater,
Wishing you could stay in bed!

Poverty!

Wanting - no longer
But needing!
With emptiness,
Hunger - heart bleeding!
Cold, tired and helpless!

Alive? Only barely!
Existing - just!
Desire? Only a memory;
Lacking in trust.
Proud, scared and angry!

Hoping for justice,
Yet fearing!
Some care and compassion,
It's joyful heart - rearing!
Just someone to care!

Searching for solace,
Finding none!
Continuous heartache,
More thirst in the sun!
Few care for the poor!

Time Is Now

Often passing, na'er a thought!
Invisible to naked eye;
If lost, cannot be ever caught,
Between our birth and day we die!

Used well, so much can be achieved,
Yet sadly, oft we squander;
It's use, is hopefully perceived,
As gaining life - much fonder!

Such waste, of thing so very rare!
Must cause great loss to every mind;
Forever after, searching where,
This priceless jewel we'll find.

Regret o'er things we've left undone,
Can ruin a fruitful day;
Thus 'do it now' beneath the sun,
Is much the better way!

Deep thought, absorbs the very wise,
In learning, when and how;
To capture such a worthy prize
And find that - Time is now!

Upwardly Mobile!

My wife and I were shopping,
At the superstore one night;
When by the chiller cabinets,
We really had a fright!

A woman talking really loud,
And laughing to herself;
It was such a great distraction,
As we looked around a shelf!

'Twas not our fault, that we could hear,
Her every secret thought;
She did not seem embarrassed,
At being so strangely caught!

We were amused by how she stood,
With laughter in our throats;
Expecting there - at any time,
Some men in clean white coats!

Yet as we passed, the woman turned,
But we had nought to fear;
Unknown to us, the woman held,
A 'mobile' to her ear!

We found that her discussion,
Was joining with a friend;
Not some inane behaviour,
Which is the current trend!

A Welcome

A welcome to Scotland, I bid you accept!
A colourful place and in general - well kept!
There are lochs that are blue and mountains of grey,
And there's heather there too! On you bonnie brae!

The scenery there, I am sure you'll enjoy,
You'll see 'Scots wha hae' full of wonder and joy!
You'll see them in freedom, wi never a fret;
You'll wander through Scotland and never forget!

There are castles and glens, rich in historic fact,
There'll be many a pageant, which they'll re-enact!
Highland Gatherings plenty - keeping you entertained;
And lots of things indoors - in case it has rained!

In those highlands and islands - variety blooms!
And you'll stay in hotels with such comfortable rooms.
If you like the outdoor life, the campsites are good,
And for those who are hungry - a rich choice in food!

The travel is easy, by bus, car or train,
And airports strategic - if you come by plane!
Scots people are friendly, in humour and jest,
Their welcome you'll relish - it will be the best!

Scots' music and drama, will set you alight,
With songs, plays and stories - well into the night!
And when the time comes, when you must go and pack,
You'll remember these joys - and you'll long to come back!

Winning Is Losing!

Winning, when you play the game,
Is what we all would choose;
Yet, isn't it an awful shame
That someone has to lose?

But, bear in mind, that taking part,
Must always meet with chance;
May upset those, whose skill, or art,
Does not their game - enhance!

So, play it well, as best you can,
And fret not - if you fall!
For losing, was not in your plan,
In play - you gave your all!

With conscience clear, you now can smile,
You lost - but passed the test!
The contest really was worthwhile,
You know, you gave your best!

David Russell

I was born in Belfast nineteen years ago, and have been living there since. My two great interests from a young age have always been art and writing, and I have recently sold some of my pictures in a gallery in Belfast.

I have been writing short stories and poems for as long as I can recall. My first poem was published by Poetry Now at the age of fourteen, and since then have been fortunate enough to have over thirty poems published in various Forward Press anthologies, in addition to three short stories. Having thoroughly enjoyed studying English literature at A-Level, I am currently an English student at Queen's University Belfast. I find that as I examine in detail the work of numerous poets, the more appreciation I have for the art of poetry.

My reason for writing poetry is a simple one - I have often found it to be an effective means of expressing feelings and ideas that I am often otherwise incapable of communicating. Much of my writing concerns darker emotions, and I often find these the most rewarding type of poem to write. As a result, themes of loss, emptiness and silence are prevalent in my writing. Although inherently bleak, I always try to discover the characteristic beauty and potential within them.

Among my many poetic influences are Ted Hughes, Seamus Heaney and Philip Larkin, and inspiration often comes from everyday occurrences, from where I endeavour to decode the inner character.

Poetry to me has become less about the specific intent of the poet and more about the importance of the reader. Reading poetry allows room for reflection and examination of the mind and thoughts, like seeing diverse shapes in clouds or pictures in inkblots. As I strive to learn more, the true reward lies in the learning, and the real poetic challenge that exists for me is the one that lies in-between the idea and the pen.

Penumbra

A cornet of ash leans in the flames
On heaped grey clots of coal and heat,
Something left, an echo of a crumpled
Page tossed sideways at the fire and peat.

I think it sad that burnt out paper
Stays the way I remember.
A grey shadow barely stands in stead,
A dead memory, a hollow ember.

Whispering its form lets us know nothing.
The iron comes stirring the coal,
Reduces to dust the steely remains,
A syndrome of glow, a fading hole.

Watching Sunday

Still water rested over the ebbed bed of toughened sand
And quenched in silence, transcending the mariner's bay
In smells of moss and orange crustaceans, against the washed sky.
Some piece of unobstructed shale and old sandcastles
Entombed in mussels were the playground for dogs
While their masters walked.
Boats crossed by on the absent tide
Below the new-launched planes and distance let me grasp
The impression of Bangor over the gentle waves.
Burying shades are beginning but sweeten the air
In hot churns of light, and wonder how and why
Their looking-glass shore is my companion.

Last Days Of Pompeii

When she died what I did first was cry,
But not for her. Then piece by piece
I forgot and struggled to recall.
I wonder why. Today I feel
There's something more to crying.
She's like the city now, there,
But mostly swallowed.

That time I wept I thought of me,
And me, alone.

There was something
Then about death that I'm finding
Now, the something that hides in
Elegies and tears, that hid in mine, and me.
It's the here and gone,
The quick and dead.
Black formed the moral panic,
Ties and shoes and feelings
Are crouched together behind
What's true, what's real about living,
And calls from graveside mourners
Let us know. But still it missed me.

As I was sitting watching morning burn,
It unveiled the weeping I'd forgotten.
For the first time since I forgot her,
I remembered what I'd not seen.

New Year

These four days were serving daggers
To flesh.
Unaccountable passion lay waste in deserts.
As lightning riddled the sands it left
The tight glass for me to look through; and
Martha's weeping heard outside Bethany.
She gave her pain to Christ.

The day is coming; and will
Break with no surprise.
In three hours, the warring winds come and go,
Discussing Armageddon under smiles,
Forgetting they are just the edges, fringes.
He brings me forth in Bethany
After the year, and its seasons.

Wave

Trembling like claws
On ravens
Newborn,
Crimped black
Feathers of hail,
Passion like snow,

Currents cascade
By it, singing,
Sweeping nettles' beauty
And chorus;
Infinite knowing,
Sepia plains
Oxidising and burning
Behind,

Pencils
Pressing its page,
Carving its tables;
Angled tins, empty,
Pots and books,
Refracted frames

Rang in chord,
Heard it.
Bits of coal, tissue,
Wood, strewn carelessly,
Falling asleep,
Racketing chances
Into the net,
Over the fence;
Blood echoed
Moon,
Ambulance noise,
Neon;

Tinkering with seasons,
Puttering confusion,
Finding no reason
There.

Cry For The Bird

Cry for the bird on that slate
As he tucks in on warmth he knows
Isn't there, but determines the
Conditions won't move him from there.
Cry for the bird bracing tight
For he wants to be sentinel,
Wants to grip high March's breath
On his pedestal, a razor-toothed slate
Placed coyly on top of the chimney.
Cry for the bird holding feathers
About him and listening for
Gulls on the shore,
And the passers ignore his persistence
That he won't be shook.
Cry for the bird that squawks
Empty virtue at a deafened wind.
His loneliest tower is the last,
For the others flew south for the summer.
Cry for the bird, for the fool
Who can't see his own life casting back
While he stands by his feathers to wait
For the passing of all shelled muttering.
He is the one glider who wrote me
A sign on a chimney pot.

When I look now I cry for the bird
Who forgot how to fly when the slate
Finally slid, and broke up like
Most life does, or must do.

Urbs Antiqua Fuit

('Barbarus hic ego sum quia non intelligor ulli')

I thronged through amoebas and drizzle
In town and trundled by watch shops and
Holes-in-walls, pacing in filth and sound,
When everything translated like conundrums and dregs,
And I found a thousand souls all with colds,
Just walking, catching the 63, whispering on acoustics,
Reading the time, following friends in the peep of dawn.
Drops nestled on my coat, like swans making their burial,
And processional fibres wept for them. Prime socks
Selling at stalls, dedicated countrymen
Flailing songs, each bit of living lost in rain.
Headlines breed murder.

Periodicals

I have found them from all public sectors,
In specialist fields down to universal disdain.
Delinquency and crime to social work practice,
I cannot waive economy and medical ethics;
Each takes part in singular purpose.

All kinds of journal are the pride of floor two
Where truancy is a thing most felt.
Bare isles with settled journals parody life.
Surely no one needs them all?
Only librarians handle each journal.

The rows fall squarely parallel
As maybe one or two engage their trail,
And something now familiar rests in this
Ignorance of who we are, or should be.
Disinterest of mind occupies enough.

But what of hidden things?
What is hidden about a current journal?
Something corrodes us when they are not
All considered. Our utopian carnival
Is trampled by utopian chains.

We deny forgotten windows when they are
Dipped into when required.
Few charter the box-shelves this morning,
The remainder discover a tumuli of journals.
How sad that we only borrow.

Candle In A Bottle

Dinner alone this night;
flames suck tight the air
and back, tight.
From the wick to new oxygen
in the green foul bottle welting wax,
sifting downwards onto nothing new;
cubist demands on the wall
above frames of unaltered women
not right on their own.
Columns mix into waiters like butterflies
and gents revelling in retirement's cocoon
smile to themselves after dinner alone.
I'm different than them,
holding beside a flaking radiator
while smelling the fire.
Outside is plagued in moons.
Restaurant homes are serenely mauve,
sorting their art by respect,
boring their customers in wine.

Autumnal Walk

In leaves gallantly imagined
in autumn's expressionist age, truant
winds brush our walking shoes
and engage her hair. She turns,
I like autumn, and *this is a nice walk.*
Moving by, eloping with yesterday's
telegraph sheet beside the twig, it
levitates the beauty of old age
and I'm motionless walking.
Old puddles and soggy leaves reflect,
pass us on our way, make me yearn for
the gooseberry spring of my childhood.
I'd love to climb that tree.

Now

I don't live here.
Clustered scraps of past and future
Being is my pinfold.
I'm the middle of the comet's stretch.

While now and again is a licence,
Yesterday and tomorrow meet
In the middle to convene my drumhead.
I don't live here.

I Became The Soft Light

I became the soft light
When my sanity took its chances.
Now I walk with no shadow
Down a platform in hours.
I'll admit to secret envy,
Their silhouettes drop like outlines
You draw on numbing trips and define
Themselves by the volume of lines.

I have no lines anymore, all she
Left me was a stain of blackness
Underneath. I disappeared
Through a gap like a fly in a bottle,
And they all see me there, pop a few
Holes in the cap to let me breathe,
But to me they seem like magnified
Wardens who hate my trembling wings.

I suspect that soft light is
What Oppenheimer was when
He shaved in a country's mirror
And found their blood in his eyes.
I saw my dark profile melt as madness
Stole away in mentally-reflected trances,
Rebounding off walls and time. I've been left
With a heap of mess and no shovel;
I dreamt last night that she was
Soft light too, this blur diffusing in etherised
Four o'clock, drowning darkly.

I crept through degrees of focus
Until I woke to the rim of reality, until
I came to grasp the nature of shadows.
I haven't got one anymore, just the
Madness of thorns.
Her shadow had left me gasping
In the terraces of chance
Before I found who she was,
Where she hid.

Untitled

Battlefields broken by a fallow wind of war
Stay barren, but not for long.
Memory has proved its fragility more than
Trench-scarred soil, sinking lower into the acid
Of unkind yesterday. Even lads of eighteen knew
Then that surrender was death.
Blood, unknown, dropping rhythmically still
Wails that death is surrender.

Time and rain fell. Trees that severed life
Breathe again through kin.
Sweeping in the south wind, flesh became grass.
One million names long forgotten built this field
And that sky. A green spring is enough to prove
Death is remembered through life.

The Raining Sun

Back-stabbers come from the grass, the turf,
Pungent moors of peat and pastel shades.

Why so?

Their grass is a dedication.

To whom?

Memorials. Should be they are saved
From extinction by existence.

A turnaround?

Of the worst kind - unhindered ignorance.
It persists through generations
Of crow's feet and money.
Grass is unaltered by its surety of fading;
Not lasting is singly its legacy.
Some bruised blades sprouted from soldiers' veins
And reminds the earth what it knows -

The sun will rain again.